TALES
OF THE
ISLE OF WIGHT

by

C. W. R. WINTER

COACH HOUSE PUBLICATIONS LTD

ISBN No. 1-899-392-092

Published by
Coach House Publications Ltd
The Coach House, School Green Road, Freshwater,
Isle of Wight, PO40 9EB

Printed by
West Island Printers Ltd, Afton Road, Freshwater,
Isle of Wight, PO40 9TT

CONTENTS

Yarmouth Castle, and the garden of the George Hotel, greet you as you enter the harbour.

YARMOUTH
ISLE OF WIGHT

ONE of the nicest possible ways of visiting the Isle of Wight is by crossing from Lymington to Yarmouth. The journey by car and passenger ferry takes 30 minutes, the ferry threading its way down the Lymington River, squeezing past the hundreds of yachts on their summer moorings, and then a short distance across the open water with the Island growing ever larger, and the sleepy old town of Yarmouth gradually taking shape. Until you are quite close the entrance to the harbour is difficult to spot, but the Castle which guards it, and the Victorian Pier alongside, soon show up.

Yarmouth was the first town in the Island to be built as such, way back in the 12th century, when its importance as a port of entry was recognised by the Norman Lord of the Island. Due to its geographical position on a peninsula of land – with the sea to the north, the River Yar to the west and extensive marshes to the south – it has never been able to sprawl in the way that has spoilt so many old English towns. Over the centuries it has managed to retain its medieval character and charm.

The Castle was built in 1545 by command of King Henry VIII who had personally witnessed the humiliating sinking of the *Mary Rose* in nearby Spithead, and who decreed that at all costs the French were to be stopped from carrying out such insulting raids. They had already sacked Yarmouth on two previous occasions, in 1377 and 1543, and the King demanded that this practice should cease forthwith. His commands were obeyed and the Castle was built, which effectively stopped the French raids, and Yarmouth was able to lick its wounds in peace. Since that time there have been no more hostile invasions of the Isle of Wight.

The ferry from Lymington docks alongside the wall of the Castle and it is worth walking along the quayside to explore this small harbour. It is full of yachts, and a modern and busy lifeboat, and there is always something going on. There are seats on the quayside, and to sit for a while and watch the movement of the boats is relaxing and therapeutic. Yarmouth seems to say "Don't worry, take it easy. There is plenty of time."

Along Quay Street towards the Square you pass The George, Yarmouth's leading hotel. This comfortable old house was rebuilt at the beginning of the 18th century from a much older building that is reputed on two occasions to have housed King John, in 1208 and 1214, when he was preparing a little invasion of his own to try and regain some of his lost French possessions.

The George, before it became an hotel, was also the home of a celebrated Governor of the Isle of Wight, Sir Robert Holmes. Holmes was a great friend of Charles II – the two men had similar tastes in wine and women – and lived here in style, conducting a piratical

Sir Robert Holmes, swashbuckling Governor of the Isle of Wight, who lived in the house which is now the George Hotel.

6

operation in the waters of the English Channel. One of the ships he captured was carrying as passenger a sculptor with an unfinished life-size white marble statue of King Louis XIV. He was travelling to the French Court in order to complete the carving of the King's head, but Holmes commandeered the statue and had his own head substituted for that of the monarch. Ever since Holmes died in 1692 the statue has proudly stood on his tomb in Yarmouth Church.

In the Square is the brick-built Town Hall, last modernised in 1763, and the seat of the Mayor since 1440. In the Reform Act of 1832 Yarmouth was deprived of its right to send two members to Parliament, one of which had been returned since 1295 and the second since 1584. The town subsequently lost its municipal status, but in the Town Hall are many treasures, relics of Yarmouth's long and illustrious past. These include a charming silver-gilt hand mace presented to the town by Charles II in 1662 in recognition of the kindness showed to his father Charles I during the latter's enforced stay in the Island in 1648.

Almost opposite the Town Hall is the Bugle Hotel, so named from the armorial bearing of Henry Beauchamp, son of the Earl of Warwick and favourite of King Henry VI, who in 1445 was for a very short time 'King' of the Isle of Wight. One of the supporters of his

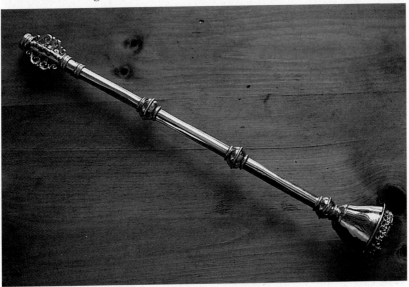

The silver gilt mace, presented to the town by Charles II in return for the kindness shown to his father, Charles I.

7

coat of arms was a young bull, called in Latin *bucullus* from which is sprung the word bugle, the connection being that a young bull and a bugle make the same sort of noise.

At the far end of the Square is the parish church of St James, and this is well worth a visit. Built in 1626 to replace two older and dilapidated buildings, and open every day as a church should be, this one exudes a great feeling of peace. It contains a number of interesting stained glass windows and other reminders of days gone by, including the statue of Sir Robert Holmes.

At the seaward end of the Square is the entrance to the Pier, itself a subject of interest as it is now the only wooden pier in England still in daily use. When restoration was carried out a few years ago money was raised by 'selling' the new planks being used in its decking, so that as you walk along you can read on the planks the carved names of the many friends who contributed to the work.

No tour of Yarmouth is quite complete without a visit to Yarmouth Mill and a short walk up the river bank along the disused railway track. The railway was closed down in 1952, which with hindsight is a great pity. It would have proved a great attraction today for its route passes through some lovely scenery, but the two miles from Yarmouth to Freshwater make a splendid walk. Near the old station is the imposing Tide Mill, now a holiday home, which

Yarmouth Harbour from the South Quay, showing the entrance and a Lymington ferry berthed by the Castle.

was built in 1793 by William Porter, who by trade was a baker of penny meat pies which he hawked round the streets. He had a brief but meteoric career as a speculative builder but lost everything when the Bank to whom he had entrusted his financial affairs closed its doors.

Yarmouth today is full of character, and is a thriving, lively and friendly community. It remembers its past with affection, but welcomes the future and whatever this may bring. As you walk through its quiet streets it is easy to imagine those early days when the town was first built, and life was less complex than it is today.

Great East Standen House today.

GREAT EAST STANDEN

I N a corner of the high chalk downs that spread across the centre of the Isle of Wight, in a little saucer-like depression that provides cover and shelter from all the winds that blow, lies the manor house of Great East Standen. Secluded and utterly peaceful, remote from the hurly-burly of everyday life, the house is nevertheless only a few short miles from Newport, the busy little county town of the Island.

The present house has no architectural aspirations. It is a pleasant, comfortable, and typically English 18th century farmhouse, fronted by a series of terraces that lead down to the drive below. On either side are stables and farm buildings and all around is the circle of the downs, making it a rather special and private place, one that the world seems to have passed by.

But Great East Standen was not always like this. Twice at least in the long and eventful history of the Isle of Wight it played an important part in Island affairs, once as the home of a Governor of the Island, and once as a refuge and safe haven for a Royal Princess, daughter of a King of England.

The earliest record of the manor of Standen is in the reign of the Saxon King Edward the Confessor, who was King of England before the Normans came. In 1066 when William of Normandy conquered England he gave the Isle of Wight to his kinsman William Fitz-Osbern, who displaced the Saxon owner of Standen and bestowed the manor on his henchman William FitzAzor.

Under the Normans the manor prospered and by the 13th century there is a record that the manor house had its own private chapel, dedicated to St Leonard, a sign that the manor had indeed grown in importance. The centuries rolled by, and 200 years later, in the year 1504, Great East Standen welcomed its most illustrious owner, the Princess Cecily, second daughter of Edward IV of England.

Edward's tenure of the throne was always precarious, and when he died in 1483 there was a great scramble for possession of the Crown. The legitimate heir was Edward's son, a boy of 13, and theoretically he became Edward V, but Richard Duke of Gloucester, his uncle, had other ideas, and was determined to seize the Crown for himself. History has recorded that Richard was an evil and unscrupulous man who let nothing stand in his way, a man to whom

11

promises were a means to an end, to be made or broken as the situation demanded.

When his brother, King Edward IV, died, Richard set himself the task of eliminating everyone who stood between him and the throne, and he naturally began with the boy king, Edward V. Ostensibly for security reasons, and swearing that no harm would come to them, Richard had the boy and his younger brother removed to the Tower of London, that grim Norman fortress in which many of the king's enemies were traditionally imprisoned, and from which very few emerged alive. No-one knows for certain what happened to the princes, but they were never seen alive again, and there is little doubt that they were murdered.

Their mother, the dowager Queen Elizabeth, had been unable to save them, and in fear for her own life, had with her five daughters fled to the Sanctuary of Westminster Abbey where they lived for some considerable time. At this time Princess Cecily was 14 years old, and the anxieties and privations of her life in these troubled months must have been very hard to bear. Richard was duly crowned king as Richard III, and ultimately persuaded Queen Elizabeth to leave the Sanctuary.

When barely 17, Princess Cecily was married off to John, Lord Wells, a man very much older than herself and not of royal blood, so that any children of the marriage would have no claim to the throne. Cecily had been betrothed once before, when she was only five years old, to the son of James III of Scotland, a contract of political convenience which was broken some years later, also for political reasons.

Richard III's reign came to a violent end in 1485 when he was killed at the Battle of Bosworth, a battle which signalled the end of the Wars of the Roses, and the accession of Henry Tudor to the throne as Henry VII. It was Henry who united the warring houses of Lancaster and York by marrying Princess Cecily's elder sister, Elizabeth. In the period of peace that followed, Cecily for the first time was able to lead a normal life. In December 1487 she and her husband attended the Court's Christmas Revels at Greenwich, and for the next ten years she lived an uneventful life and gave birth to two daughters.

Her husband died in 1498 leaving her a very rich woman. She was 29 years old. In 1501 there is another record of her attending the Revels, this time in celebration of the marriage of Arthur, Prince of Wales to Catherine of Aragon, and it is noted that she performed two dances with the bridegroom.

But the 'high society' life of the Court had never been an attraction to Princess Cecily. The troubles and dangers experienced during her formative years had left their scars and she was never able completely to relax. Both her daughters died when quite young, and it must have seemed to her that life was a series of blow after cruel blow, and that happiness and true content had once again eluded her.

And then in 1503 came a change. She met, fell in love with, and married Sir Richard Keene who lived in the Isle of Wight, and who was described by Sir John Oglander, the Island historian, as 'very personable, and a proper man'. On her marriage she left the Court with all its superficial attractions and came to live at Great East Standen as the wife of a typical country gentleman. Perhaps in the peace and quiet of this secluded spot she at last found the stability and happiness that she had sought for so long.

Alas though, this state was not destined to last, for on 24th August 1507 she died, after something less than four years in her new home. Her death created quite a stir in the Island where, as a daughter of Edward IV, she had been held in great reverence. The Abbot of Quarr, the great Cistercian Abbey in the north of the Island, requested the honour and privilege of burying her in his Abbey, and this was granted.

The funeral was attended by a number of the gentry of the Island, and on this day many monks from Quarr, followed by the mourners, escorted the body from Great East Standen to the Abbey. As the cortège wound its way along the pleasant country lanes through Downend and Briddlesford, tapers were burned and prayers for the dead were recited. Sir John Oglander wrote that the interment was carried out with all honour and state by the Convent and gentry of the whole Island, and the Lord Abbot preached at her funeral. She was buried in the midst of the great Abbey Church, as befitted the daughter of a King and the sister of a Queen.

Her grave is regrettably now lost, along with those of other notabilities of past ages, for in 1536 the Abbey of Quarr was closed by order of Henry VIII, and within the next year or so the Church was demolished and the stones sold for building purposes to all and sundry. In the 19th century, when Queen Victoria came to live in the Isle of Wight, an attempt was made to locate the grave, since she believed that a Royal Princess should not be allowed to lie in an unknown tomb, but to no avail.

The Queen asked a celebrated Island architect and antiquarian, Percy Goddard Stone, to visit Quarr and investigate, but this little plan did not work. Quarr at this time was occupied by a group of French monks who had acquired the ruins and were busy building the new Abbey. Unfortunately they knew no English and Stone could not speak French, so there was a language problem, and the monks completely misunderstood the purpose of his mission. Stone is known to have been slightly irascible, and apparently he did not get on very well with the monks, who finally reminded him some-what brusquely that they were monks and that there were absolutely no women there at all!

The site of Princess Cecily's grave in the ruins of the original Quarr Abbey.

Almost a hundred years after Princess Cecily's death, Great East Standen was again in the limelight, this time as the home of another celebrity, a flamboyant Governor of the Island, very different from the shy and retiring Princess, but equally interesting.

Henry Wriothesley, 3rd Earl of Southampton, led a somewhat spectacular life, often in trouble, and experiencing both the heights of success and the depths of disgrace. His colourful life story has been described in the booklet "Colourful Characters of the Isle of Wight", for Henry Wriothesley was certainly one of the most highly coloured of all the 'characters' who have graced this Island. And there have been many who have brought the glare of publicity to this quiet place by reason of their influence on affairs of state. It is in fact remarkable how this small off-shore island has repeatedly found itself on the fringe of momentous events.

Henry Wriothesley, whether as a flamboyant and unconventional Governor, or as a friend of the disaster prone Earl of Essex, or as a lover of William Shakespeare, was never far from the news of the day. He liked to live dangerously, and though he spent many years in the Isle of Wight and became popular with the gentry through his regular invitation to play bowls, he ultimately found the quiet life too tame and returned to a more war-like occupation, which unfortunately led to his death.

The 3rd Earl's bowling green?

A local historian, writing about him 200 years later, said:

> "It has been transmitted to posterity that he was just, affable, and obliging in his deportment to all; that he was universally esteemed by all ranks of people; that the Island was raised to a flourishing state by his mild and condescending deportment, and that many gentlemen of great affluence and hospitality were induced to reside there during this period."

The splendid view eastwards from the Down above Great East Standen.

On the 3rd Earl's departure from the Island in 1624, Great East Standen relaxed and returned to its accustomed peaceful existence, slumbering once more in its quiet little pocket of the Downs, a tranquil haven that successive owners have been able to enjoy. Who knows when it will next be disturbed from its sleep? Who will be the next to bring it back to the centre of the Island stage?

Swainston House and the Bishops' Chapel.

MUSIC AT SWAINSTON

THE late Norman Thurston, who played such an active part in the musical life of the Island, and who has left us with so many happy memories, organised in 1987 a series of concerts in the Bishops' Chapel at Swainston Manor. These were deservedly popular and were invariably sold out.

The Bishops' Chapel is a venerable building of great age and was originally built by the Bishops of Winchester who created Swainston as their summer palace in Saxon times. The room has played its part in the history of the Isle of Wight, and indeed of England, and no better place could have been found as a venue for the concerts.

A short talk on some aspect of this Island history was given at each concert, and the following three-part article covers the last one of these, and describes three different and significant events in the history of the room.

A Talk given at a Concert on 5th September 1987

– Part I –

Tonight I want you to use your imagination. I want to talk about this room (The Bishops' Chapel), and I want to recreate – with your help, and the help of your imagination – three occasions in the history of this room. Most of you will know that at one time this room was the private Oratory or Chapel of the Bishops of Winchester, that it was part of their 'Summer Palace' in the Isle of Wight, and that they owned it, and loved it, and relaxed in it – and worshipped in it – for over 500 years, until they lost it in 1286.

The first date I want to conjure up out of the past is 5th November, 1285. November 5th has a familiar sound, and most of you will immediately think of fireworks and bonfires and Guy Fawkes, but in 1285 the events of the Gunpowder Plot which gave us our traditional excitement on this date were still 320 years away. At this time, in 1285, England still had only one religion, one form of religious observance, a form which we know today as Roman Catholicism.

But the excitement here at Swainston, and in this room, on 5th November, 1285, was far greater than could ever be generated by fireworks and bonfires, for on this day they were awaiting the arrival of no less a person than the King of England himself ,Edward I, who was coming to stay for six days. Even the humblest of his subjects knew all about King Edward; his fame had spread throughout the whole of the civilised world, his exploits on the Crusades and in the many battles he had fought in France and against the Welsh were talked about in every cottage in his Kingdom.

He was known and admired for his bravery and intelligence, he was feared for his cruelty and ferocity against any who disputed his will, he was at once the most respected and most feared King the English had had since the days of the Conqueror. Edward I was revered for the many good laws he had given to England, as for instance the clearing of ground to one bowshot length on either side of the main highways, which made travel so much safer. He was respected for his development of the English Parliamentary system and his founding of the House of Commons. He was feared for his savage persecution and plundering of the Jews, and for the terrible punishment he invented for traitors – the death by being hung, drawn, and quartered.

So his arrival at Swainston was awaited with mixed feelings, and his host the Bishop of Winchester, the Right Reverend John di Pontiserra, was understandably nervous. Why was the King honouring him with this visit? Why wasn't he going to stay at Carisbrooke Castle, the seat of the Owner of the Isle of Wight, the Lady Isabella de Fortibus? John di Pontiserra – who in spite of his Italian sounding name was an Englishman, John Sawbridge – knew that his own position was a bit tricky. He had been appointed to the See of Winchester, not by the King, but by the Pope, and he knew that the King was displeased. He was also well aware that to upset a man as powerful and unscrupulous as Edward I was a very dangerous proceeding.

So the situation at Swainston was tense. When the King and his numerous followers and men-at-arms arrived they were automatically offered refreshment, but once the requirements of hospitality had been attended to the King desired to offer up a prayer for his safe arrival. Travel in those days was an uncertain business, and even the crossing of the Solent in a small boat was by no means without peril. What was this Chapel like in those days? It would of course be much plainer and barer than it is today. The walls would not have been plastered and painted, but have been bare stone. There would have been no carpet on the floor, only rushes. Rushes, which in all probability would have been gathered from the marshes of nearby Newtown. The windows would not have been glazed –

The Chapel built by a Bishop of Winchester many centuries ago.

glass for windows not becoming general until the 14th century – but they would have been fitted with shutters to keep out most, though not all, of the weather. The beautiful east window, which is now such a feature of this room, was probably not there. There would be no seats, with the exception perhaps of a stool or two – for the Bishop, and of course the King. There would be no heating.

So on this November day in 1285 this Chapel would have presented a bleak and very different appearance. The shutters to the windows on the south and west side would be closed to keep out the November wind and rain, and those on the north side would not let in enough light completely to dispel the gloom. There would of course be candles of many different sizes, and possibly crude torches held in wall sconces, but these would be flickering and guttering in the cold and draughty air.

As the Bishop's Chaplain intoned the Latin prayers, and acolytes swung censors to and fro, filling the air with the heavy perfume of the incense, what thoughts would be passing through the heads of the King and the Bishop as they knelt side by side on the rushes? Were they able to concentrate on their devotions, or were their earthly problems too strong to be pushed aside? The Bishop was no doubt concerned about his duties as host to this unfriendly and fearsome monarch, and was apprehensive about the real meaning of the King's visit and its effect on his own future. It is unlikely that the

King gave much thought at this time to the job he had come to do, namely to take away from the Bishop this valuable and strategically important manor of Swainston. He was probably more worried about immediate problems, such as how soon he could get up off his knees, and what was he going to be offered for supper. Business about the manor could wait until tomorrow.

When the short service came to an end, the Bishop rose to his feet to pronounce the benediction. In the flickering and failing light his features looked strained as he made the sign of the Cross and called upon God to bless his sovereign and all those assembled there, in the name of the most Holy and Blessed Trinity – *Benedicant Omnipotens Deus, Pater, et Filius, et Spiritus Sanctus.*

– Part II –

The second day I want to bring back to life is a very different kind of day. The 25th July 1588 was a hot day, a perfect summer's day, a day when the sun shone down out of a cloudless blue sky, when the sea around the Island was Mediterranean blue in colour, and indeed when the Island itself was still and calm, and at its beautiful best.

But the day was one of mixed emotions in the Isle of Wight – apprehension and fear in the morning, though by the afternoon this had changed to relief and thanksgiving.

On 5th July a small ship had sailed into Portsmouth – the 80 ton *Rat of Wight*, commanded by Captain Gilbert Leigh, a member of a well-known Island family. He reported that he had come from Spain as fast as his sails could carry him, and that on the day he left a great Spanish Armada had also set sail for England, bent on invasion. His information was that they were heading for the Isle of Wight.

This invasion had been threatening, on and off, for the last 30 years, and indeed could well have matured in the previous year had not Sir Francis Drake taken the initiative and raided Cadiz harbour where he destroyed valuable stores, and a large stock of seasoned barrel staves. The latter were a vital part of their invasion preparations, as all the Armada's food and water had to be carried in casks, and the destruction of these barrel staves actually caused a 12 month delay.

In the Island, preparations to meet the expected onslaught had reached fever pitch. Since the appointment of Sir George Carey as Captain of the Island in 1582, the Home Guard, or Militia, had practised assiduously and were comfortingly efficient. They numbered altogether 1,856 officers and men, 1,158 armed with muskets, 109 archers, 116 pikemen, and 473 with halberds or bills. Although they expected to be vastly outnumbered, they were determined to give a good account of themselves.

At dawn on Thursday 25th July the Armada was within sight of the Isle of Wight, but they were becalmed. They numbered 130 ships, many of them huge and bristling with troops preparing to land on Island beaches. Behind the Spaniards to the west lay the English fleet, all 54 of them, but smaller and faster than the unwieldy Spanish galleons. During the morning, as the two navies slowly drifted eastwards, the English managed to prevent the Spaniards from entering the Needles Channel, and an invasion of the Island was thus averted,

Here in Swainston all was excitement. In the morning, as soon as the news was received that the Armada could be seen, horses were saddled and a party left for the Downs between Freshwater and Brook. The sight that met their eyes was truly breathtaking. The whole surface of the sea seemed to be covered by the huge crescent of Spanish ships, slowly and majestically making their way eastwards under the gradually increasing breeze, with the smaller and faster English ships harrying and worrying them, snapping at their heels like a pack of terriers.

As the morning wore on it became apparent to the watchers on the shore that the immediate danger to the Island was past. There was going to be no invasion that day, and the feeling of apprehension and tension gradually gave way to a great wave of relief and relaxation. The Swainston party turned for home.

In the afternoon the Reverend Nicholas Udall, Vicar of Calbourne, arrived to conduct a service of praise and thanksgiving for deliverance from the threat of invasion that had hung over the Island for so long. Here in this very room the house party gathered, from the Owner, Sir Thomas Barrington and his wife, Lady Winifred, down to the youngest housemaid and the newest stable boy who had only been taken on two weeks before.

As the sunlight flooded into this Chapel the Priest's final words at the conclusion of the service fell like a blessing on all those present:

> "God preserve our Queen and realm this day and for evermore, and send us truth and quietness within ourselves."

East end of the Chapel and the 13th century church type window.

– Part III –

The third day I want to talk about is again very different to the other two. Mainly because it brings us nearer to the present time. The first two days described occasions in which this room was host to well-known and even famous people. On both these occasions it was subject to powerful emotions – emotions that ranged from apprehension and fear to joy and thankfulness. The emotions on this third day are possibly not as strong, but nevertheless are important, for they are all part of the continuing history of the room, a history that has been going on day after day, night after night, for something like a thousand years.

Some of you may have already guessed that the third day I want to talk about is a Saturday. Not just any old Saturday, but Saturday 5th September 1987. In other words – tonight.

The room has changed vastly in appearance since those early days in the 13th century. It now has neatly plastered and painted walls, it has concealed electric lighting, it has a fitted carpet, and comfortably upholstered seats for those who use it. It is embellished with beautiful flower arrangements. But it is still the same room that the Bishops of Winchester used as a Chapel for over 500 years. It is still the same room that has been owned by many famous people – Dukes, Earls, Countesses, Baronets and Knights – all of whom have contributed something of their own personalities to the atmosphere of the room, culminating in the present owners, Fred and Margaret Woodward, by whose kind permission we have been able to use it for our concerts.

What are we like – the people who are occupying this room tonight, and who are thus contributing to and continuing the history of this ancient Chapel of the once Royal Manor of Swainston?

Here I must obviously be careful. I must not draw too much attention to the pretty girl in the second row from the back, nor to the gentleman in the third row from the front who is so desperately trying to keep awake. Perhaps I should not even draw attention to the talented musicians who have already entertained us, and who are waiting so patiently to continue the concert.

We are perhaps a pretty average bunch of people, all drawn together here tonight for a common purpose – to enjoy good music, well played, and in surroundings the antiquity of which ensures an ambience which is unsurpassed in the Island. Our occupation tonight is, I am sure, one that accords well with the history of this room, and one of which John di Pontiserra, one time Bishop of

Another very old window with a modern embellishment.

Winchester, would thoroughly approve. I like to think so; and who knows but that the shades of all these people who have gone before us are here with us tonight. And who knows what the years to come have in store for this room? Let us hope that it may see many years of happiness, and that others like us may meet here and be entertained.

And now perhaps I may be permitted to conclude these random remarks on the occasion of this, the last concert in the series, with the heartfelt saying of Charles Dickens' character, Tiny Tim – "God Bless us all, everyone."

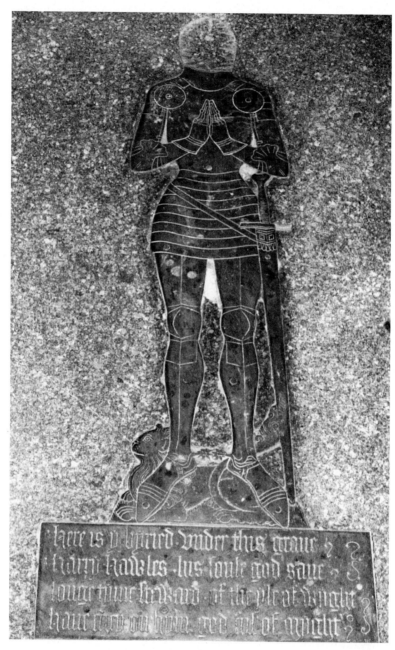

The brass marking the grave of Harry Hawles in Arreton Church,
Isle of Wight.

THE BATTLE ON
ST CRISPIN'S DAY

HARRY HAWLES lived in the Isle of Wight in the early years of the 15th century. He was one of the men-at-arms that fought with King Henry V in his continental campaign to recover the lost English possessions in France, a campaign that began in August 1415 with the capture of the town of Harfleur, and culminated with the battle of Agincourt on October 25th, St Crispin's Day.

The campaign was dominated by the bravery and leadership of the young king, whose stirring battle-cry before the walls of Harfleur was, in Shakespeare's words: "Cry God for Harry, England, and St George!" Harry Hawles must have been proud to have the same name as his king who inspired his pitifully small force to deeds of incredible valour.

The reduction of the fortress of Harfleur was not achieved without enormous cost, for sickness broke out in the English camp and practically halved the size of King Henry's army, and by the time he had garrisoned the town and set off on the 160 mile march to Calais, he was left with less than 6,000 men in total. On the way the King had to cope with the mighty French army which has been variously estimated as containing up to 100,000 men.

They met near the little village of Agincourt, and the most extraordinary battle ever fought by an English army developed. The French were so sure of victory that they repeatedly sent heralds to King Henry offering him terms for surrender, the last envoy being a knight, the Sire de Helly, who had once been a prisoner in England, and was accused of breaking his parole. This man offered to fight single-handed any man in the English army who dared to question his honour.

"Sir Knight," said Henry, curtly, "this is no time for single combat. Go, tell your countrymen to prepare for battle, and doubt not that, for the violation of your word, you shall a second time forfeit your liberty if not your life."

"Sir," replied de Helly, insolently, "I will receive no orders from you. Charles is our sovereign. Him we will obey, and for him we will fight against you whenever we think proper."

"Away then," said Henry, "and take care that we are not before you!"

Immediately he sounded the 'advance' and the English army moved forward until they were within bowshot of the French. Five thousand of the English force were archers, and the French from past experience had learned to be wary of them, for they knew that the English long bow was capable of winning battles.

Then every Englishman knelt down and kissed the ground, a custom they had learned from the Flemish who in a previous battle with the French had obtained a brilliant victory after each man had taken up a particle of earth in his mouth, while the priest in front elevated the Host. It was a sign of consecration to the great duty of the day, and the English archers then rose from their knees and with a great shout loosed off their first volley of arrows, with devastating effect.

The battle then rapidly became a shambles. There had been much rain and the ground between the two armies soon was a quagmire in which the French horses could not keep their footing, and the French knights in their heavy army could not stand up. Thousands were suffocated, and thousands more were despatched by the English as they lay helpless on the ground. At the end of the day the French had lost 10,000 killed, and 14,000 had been taken prisoner. The rest made good their escape. The English losses were very small, the highest estimate being 1,600, but one contemporary writer claimed there were only 40.

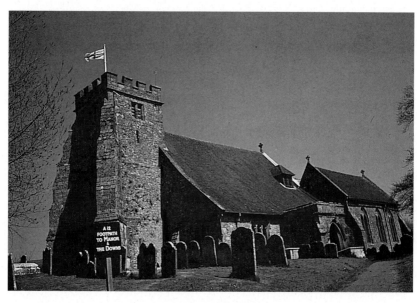

The Church of St George, Arreton.

Henry steadfastly refused to accept the credit for this astounding victory, saying it was entirely God's doing, but the jubilation not only in the English army but throughout the whole nation can be imagined. Shakespeare later immortalised the event in *The Life of King Henry V*.

In this play, a few hours before the battle, Henry has occasion to reprove one of his comrades, the Earl of Westmoreland, for wishing they had a few more thousand men with them:

"God's will! I pray thee, wish not one man more:
By Jove, I am not covetous for gold,
Nor care I who doth feed upon my cost;
It yearns me not if men my garments wear,
Such outward things dwell not in my desires;
But, if it be a sin to covet honour,
I am the most offending soul alive.
O, do not wish one more!
Rather proclaim it Westmoreland, through my host,
That he which hath no stomach for this fight,
Let him depart; his passport shall be made,
And crowns for convoy put into his purse:
We would not die in that man's company,
That fears his fellowship to die with us.
This day is called – the feast of Crispian;
He that outlives this day, and comes safe home,
Will stand a tip-toe when this day is named,
And rouse him at the name of Crispian.
He that outlives this day, and sees old age,
Will yearly on the vigil feast his neighbours,
And say – Tomorrow is Saint Crispian:
Then will he strip his sleeve and show his scars,
And say – These wounds I had on Crispin's day,
Old men forget; yet all shall be forgot,
But he'll remember with advantages
What feats he did that day. Then shall our names
Be in his flowing cups freshly remembered.
This story shall the good man teach his son,
But we in it shall be remembered:
We few, we happy few, we band of brothers;
For he today who sheds his blood with me,
Shall be my brother; be he never so vile,
This day shall gentle his condition;

The flag of St George of England proudly flies over Arreton Church.

> And gentlemen in England, now abed,
> Shall think themselves accurs'd they were not here;
> And hold their manhoods cheap, while any speaks
> That fought with us upon St Crispin's Day."

Harry Hawles came safe home from Agincourt, and returned to the Isle of Wight. He lived for another 15 years, and in those years how many times he must have stripped his sleeve and shown his scars. When he died, in 1430, he was buried with honour in the parish church of Arreton, in the Island, and over his grave was placed a brass of a knight in armour with the following inscription:

> Here is y buried under this grave
> Harry Hawles, his soul God save,
> long tyme steward of the Yle of Wyght,
> have mercie on hym, God full of myght.

The grave and the brass are still there, and the church appropriately enough is dedicated to St George, Patron Saint of England.

The church on Godshill dominates this ancient village.

AN ENGLISH ISLAND VILLAGE

WE all have our own mental picture of the typical old English village, and though these pictures may vary they all have certain features in common, such as thatched cottages with roses round the door, a medieval church, and a village inn with low ceilings, oak beams, and log fires. Godshill in the Isle of Wight has all these qualifications and much more besides, for it also has character, a long history, and a genuine welcome to visitors. Looking down on the village from the top of Church Hill, and dominating it, is the magnificent 14th century church of All Saints.

Godshill Church is a delight. It is the largest pre-Reformation church in the Island, and it attracts visitors as jam attracts wasps. It is believed that the hill on which it stands originally contained a pagan shrine, and there is a legend attaching to the first Christian church which was built in the middle of the 11th century. This church was planned for a site about a mile to the south, and work actually began, but each night the stones that had been laid were mysteriously moved from the site and deposited on top of the hill. After three nights the builders accepted this as a divine hint and decided to build their church on the hill, thus giving the village its name of Godshill. And there the church has stood ever since, the present building being the fourth in the series.

The church is often referred to as 'the Church of the Lily Cross' due to a beautiful 15th century mural in the south transept depicting Christ crucified on a triple branched flowering lily. The mural has only survived by a lucky accident, for at the time of the Reformation it was white-washed over in the general hysteria surrounding the new belief that all such pictorial representations were idolatrous. Not until the white-wash began to peel off in the middle of the 19th century was it rediscovered. It has been skillfully restored and is a work of great beauty. The Lily Cross is also unique to Godshill, there being none other like it in the British Isles.

At the Norman Conquest in 1066 Godshill was one of six Isle of Wight churches given to the Abbey of Lyre in Normandy by the new Norman Lord of the Island, and for the next 400 years the Abbey remained in control, enjoying the tithes and rents from this very prosperous parish. Due to the frequency with which England and

France were at war with each other during this period, the Abbey did not find control of its Isle of Wight properties at all easy, and there were times when there were eruptions of violence. For example, in 1308 armed monks from the Abbey of Lyre had to

The unique 15th century Lily Cross.

defend the church against the introduction of a new Rector who had been nominated by the Bishop of Winchester, and indeed was the latter's cousin.

But Godshill has other claims to fame besides its beautiful tourist-happy church, for the local estate of Appuldurcombe Park belonged for several hundred years to two of the Island's most distinguished families, the Leighs and the Worsleys. Sir John Leigh of Flamston in Wiltshire came to the Isle of Wight early in the 16th century, and married Agnes Fry of Appuldurcombe who was a rich young widow. There is an old saying that you should not marry for money, but that it is not a bad idea to marry where the money is, and this is exactly what John Leigh did, for Agnes was the richest woman in the Island and the owner of extensive lands.

Their marriage was fruitful and produced two daughters, but John Leigh did not live to old age to enjoy his wealth, for in 1523 he suffered an unfortunate accident. When out riding one day his horse stumbled over a wild boar and threw him, and in falling he broke his neck. They buried him in Godshill Church in a magnificent tomb, which still remains the finest in the Island, and when his widow died two years later they buried her alongside him. On top of the tomb they erected alabaster effigies of the knight and his lady, with his feet resting symbolically on the back of a wild boar whose head is turned as if looking round at him and saying: "I didn't do it on purpose – it was a pure accident!" The soles of Sir John's feet are carved in the likeness of two monks telling their beads, and they are indeed known as 'the bedesmen', the whole concept being a sort of medieval joke, for they are praying for his soul.

Of Sir John's two daughters, the elder one, Isobel, became a nun and renounced worldly wealth, so that the younger one, Anne, inherited all the Appuldurcombe fortune. In due course she met and married a young courtier, Sir James Worsley, and these two founded the Worsley dynasty which practically ruled the Isle of Wight up to the beginning of the 19th century.

When he was a boy, James Worsley had served as a Page at the court of King Henry VII. As luck would have it he was the same age as Prince Henry who later became Henry VIII, and at this time there was a curious law making it a crime physically to hit a prince of the royal blood. This meant that if Prince Henry did anything wrong – and he was just as prone to misdemeanors as anyone else – he could not be punished in the normal way. Everyone realised that this was a regrettable situation, and indeed when Henry grew up it was apparent that a few beatings as a boy would have done him a world of good, but there was little that could be done about it. Except, and this was felt to be the only possible solution, to elect a boy of the same age to be a 'whipping boy', who could take the punishment in lieu of the Prince.

James Worsley became this whipping boy. There is no record of how many whackings he took on behalf of his royal colleague, but they did him no harm at all. The only harm done was to Prince Henry who got away with much, and grew up to be arrogant, self-willed and undisciplined. But nevertheless he was grateful, and when he became King he knighted James, made him Yeoman of the Wardrobe, an important post at a Tudor Court, and ultimately appointed him Captain and Governor of the Isle of Wight. Which is a very good example of another old saying, that it is not *what* you know that is important but *who*.

Sir James Worsley lived to a good age and ultimately, together with his wife, was also buried in Godshill Church. His memorial is not quite as elaborate as that of his father-in-law Sir John Leigh, but nevertheless it is rather splendid and worthy of attention. Like all the other memorials in this church it is in immaculate condition.

The tomb of Sir James and Lady Anne Worsley.

38

In due course their elder son Richard followed his father as Captain of the Island, and had the honour of entertaining King Henry VIII at Appuldurcombe. The King did not enjoy his visit for he had been promised good hawking in the Island with a plentiful supply of pheasants and partridges. Unfortunately, there were none to be found, and the King was not pleased. He returned to London in a rather grumpy mood, and in his thank you letter – if such it can be described – he warned Richard that next time he came he would expect more game – or else . . .

Richard was a good Captain, and did much to strengthen the defences of the Island, building fortifications on the coast at Sandown, Cowes and Yarmouth. He re-vitalised the Militia, arming them with firearms, which at the time was thought to be a very progressive move. He instituted more rigorous training for the Militia, and insisted that every parish should not only acquire a cannon but should become proficient in its use. He also served his King well, as Commissioner for the Collection of Church Plate, under which umbrella he plundered and closed down the local Cistercian Monastery at Quarr. He married and had two sons, neither of whom reached maturity, for shortly after their father's death in 1565 they were both tragically killed in a gunpowder accident. Richard also fathered an illegitimate boy whose mother was his dairymaid and who, according to contemporary accounts, was 'a good handsome wench'.

The family fortunes prospered, however, and in 1604 another Richard inherited Appuldurcombe. This second Richard married a very beautiful woman, Frances Neville, whose father had influence at Court and obtained for his son-in-law firstly a knighthood and then a baronetcy, and this firmly established the Worsleys among the ranks of the aristocracy.

Sir Richard, the first baronet, was a strange character. He had the misfortune to lose the sight of one eye in a hunting accident as a boy and this rather put him off such energetic sports. In their place he developed the pastime of inviting a few friends to his house for the purpose of flinging cushions at each other, but alas this also had to be given up when one day he was hit in his good eye with a cushion, and for a moment thought he was completely blinded.

The fourth baronet, Sir Robert Worsley, married in his twenties a daughter of Viscount Weymouth and proceeded to build a large new Palladian mansion at Appuldurcombe. Regrettably this is now in a semi-ruinous condition, having been rendered roofless and windowless by a bomb in the second world war, but even so it is still

39

One of the cherubs guarding the tomb of Sir Robert Worsley and his brother Henry.

an architectural treasure. Sir Robert's brother Henry died, and Robert erected a rather ostentatious memorial to him in Godshill Church, and just in case no-one thought of doing the same for him when he came to die he took the precaution of including himself in the memorial to brother Henry. The result is not particularly pleasing to the modern eye, though no doubt perfectly acceptable at the time, but the monument is protected by two little cherubs whose expressions suggest that they too were not entirely in favour.

The last Worsley to live in Appuldurcombe House and to be commemorated in Godshill Church was the seventh Baronet, another Sir Richard. He led a moderately tempestuous life, being somewhat wild in his youth and having the wherewithal to indulge his every whim. He became a celebrated art collector, filling his house with beautiful things, money being in plentiful supply. One of the beautiful things was his wife, a rich society beauty of seventeen when they married in 1775. Unfortunately, she proved to be a nymphomaniac and this ultimately led to disaster. Richard turned a blind eye to many of her romantic adventures, but when she finally eloped with one of her numerous lovers he felt it was time to call a halt. He sued her paramour for £20,000, and the resulting High Court action caused quite a lot of dirty linen to be washed in public. Lady Worsley was accused of having had 35 lovers, a claim she hotly denied, but 27 of these charges stuck, and the judge had no hesitation in finding in favour of Sir Richard, and awarded him damages. Not the £20,000 he had asked for, but only one shilling, which was the judge's estimate of the value of this beautiful creature.

When Sir Richard died in 1805 his wealth passed to a nephew who in an excess of gratitude for this great good fortune erected an expensive memorial in the church to his uncle. This consisted of a huge sarcophagus with claw feet mounted on a plinth, and it is without doubt the most revoltingly vulgar monument in the whole church. A subsequent vicar so hated the sight of it that he had it moved from its position in the centre of the south transept and tucked it discreetly behind the organ where the curious can still get at it. Local people have irreverently dubbed it 'the bath'.

Godshill village has survived the Worsley regime, and during the present century has become a Mecca for Island visitors. It specialises now in holiday souvenirs and cream teas, and its several attractive tea gardens are havens of rest for tourists with tired feet. The church is still the focal point of the village. It looks down benignly from its perch on the top of God's hill, as it has done for many hundreds of years. There is no reason why it should not continue for many more.

The old church tower of St Helens stands sentinel over the bay.

HOLYSTONES

THE little village of St Helens in the Isle of Wight slumbers peacefully in the sunshine, remembering the days when it was famous and known throughout the world to sailors of all nations. When the prevailing sou-westerly winds rise to gale force and lash the coasts of the Island, which they very often do, the waters off St Helens remain calm, sheltered in the lee of the Island, and for this reason St Helens Roads became popular as a resort for shipping. Not only from those seeking shelter until the weather abated, but also for ships waiting for a fair wind down Channel, for sailing ships could not sail into a head wind.

But St Helens possessed two other attractions to shipmasters in the days of sail, one of these being the quality of the drinking water in its wells. Water was always a problem on long, slow voyages for it tended very quickly to become brackish and unpalatable. St Helens water, however, had been found through long experience to be particularly pure, and to have exceptional keeping qualities, and this prompted many a shipmaster to fill his water breakers here whenever the opportunity served.

The other attraction was its holystones, so called because they came from a church. Way back in the 11th century this quiet little bay had seen the founding of a small Priory, and the church itself had been built on the edge of the low cliffs overlooking the sea. Legend has it that the founder was a monk who came from Chichester, only a few miles away on the mainland, and he positioned his church so that from the top of the tower he could see his native town of which he had fond memories.

The Priory was sponsored by the French Abbey of Cluny, and this ultimately led to its downfall, for in 1414, at the outbreak of one of the innumerable wars between this country and France, it was suppressed, along with three other similar religious foundations in the Isle of Wight. When the monks departed, the church was taken over by the village, and for the next 300 years it served as the parish church. But alas it had been built too near the edge of the cliff, and by the 18th century erosion had undermined it to such an extent that it had to be abandoned. A new church was built a mile inland and the old one was allowed to collapse, only the tower surviving. This was retained and preserved as a seamark, where it remains to this day in defiance of the elements, and as a reminder of once glorious days.

All that remains of the 11th century church.

The popularity of St Helens as a haven for shipping reached its climax in the 18th century and then declined, although even today ships can be seen anchored in the Roads waiting for an improvement in the weather. In its hey-day it achieved national importance through being adopted by the Royal Navy as a principal marshalling point, and the Navy of the day had a fearsome reputation. The Press Gangs roamed the streets of the towns looking for 'volunteers', the discipline afloat and ashore was shudderingly stern, and the standard of 'spit and polish' aboard ship was known and marvelled at throughout the land.

One of the Navy's proudest boasts was of the meticulously spotless condition of its ships' decks, and this is where the St Helens holystones come into the picture. Decks were scoured by using sharp sand as an abrasive, this being obtained from the beach and being applied to the decks by means of heavy stones dragged to and fro by perspiring sailors. The abandoned stones from the old Priory church were found to be ideal for the purpose, and the word 'holystones' came into the English language. Holystoning the decks was by no means a popular chore, and indeed the lower decks coined their own little couplet concerning it:

"Six days shalt thou labour and do all that thou art able,
And on the seventh holystone the decks and scrape the cable."

So, what with water and grit, St Helens contributed to the efficiency of a Navy that became respected and feared by the whole world. Well may the little tower of the old Priory church sit on the seashore basking in the sunshine and remembering its past.

*'Holy' stones found on the beach
below the church tower.*

The White Horse Inn, Whitwell, one of the oldest pubs on the Island, built 1454. Could there have been an alehouse here to refresh travellers of an even earlier age?

THE TIN TRADE

IN my book "The Enchanted Isle" mention is made of the possibility that the Romans operated a regular trade in tin from the Cornish mines, bringing it along the south coast, crossing to the Isle of Wight, carrying it through the Island to Niton, shipping it to France, and then down through France to Marseilles. This possibility has intrigued historians for centuries, and many opinions have been expressed, ranging from the 'absolutely certain' to the 'quite impossible'. So what is the truth? Was there once a Tin Trade many years ago that involved the Isle of Wight, or was it all in the imagination, built up from scraps of circumstantial evidence and strange coincidences into a plausible theory? Let us have a look at the evidence and see what we can deduce, for though it may not be convincing, it is certainly interesting.

It all began a very long time before the Roman occupation of Britain, in fact round about 1100 B.C. At this time, we are told, the Greek name for what is now the British Isles was *Cassiterides*, which means the Tin Islands, and that the Greeks and Phœnicians visited the Islands to collect the metal. Later the name Cassiterides became restricted to mean the Scilly Isles and Cornwall, where large deposits of cassiterite or tinstone were to be found.

Many ancient writers have referred to the Tin Islands, and to the trade carried out with the Mediterranean nations, one of the first being the historian Herodotus, who was born c. 484, and who mentions the Phœnicians and Greeks being involved in the trade in 450 B.C. Phœnicia was a small state in what is now Lebanon, the principal cities being Tyre and Sidon, and the Phœnicians were renowned as sailors. For centuries they were regarded as the general carriers and traders of Europe. What is of especial interest in this present discussion is that the Phœnicians of Tyre founded a colony on the north African coast (in what is now Tunisia), and this colony and city, which was called Carthage, became one of the most prosperous trading ports in the Mediterranean, rivalling the Greek port of Marseilles, and also Rome itself.

The Greeks of Marseilles were in particular competition with the Phœnicians of Carthage for the tin trade, this rivalry being authenticated by the writings of the traveller Pytheas, c. 350 B.C., who because of his skill as a mathematician and navigator was engaged by the Greeks of Marseilles to help them sail to Britain. This testimony from a man who claims to have visited Britain and to have been involved in the trade is certainly interesting. Another Greek writer, Polybius, who was born c. 204 B.C., and who visited Britain c. 160 B.C., has also referred to the tin trade. Both Pytheas and Polybius wrote extensively about their travels and about Britain, and though much of their work has unfortunately been lost, enough has survived to establish that there certainly was a trade in tin with the Tin Islands in ancient times. What their writings do not prove, however, is that the Tin Islands were in fact the Scillies and Cornwall, some scholars claiming that the *Cassiterides* were located in Spain.

Carthage became so prosperous and powerful that Rome felt threatened, and in 146 B.C. the Romans attacked Carthage and destroyed it, demolition of the city being utterly brutal and complete, no trace of it having survived. Their other trading rival, Marseilles, was captured from the Greeks in the conquest of Gaul, leaving the Romans in complete control of the western Mediterranean, and it is at this time that they are alleged to have taken over the tin trade.

Two other Greek writers, Diodorous Siculous and Strabo, who both lived in the first century B.C., have written about the trade and about Britain. Diodorus Siculous wrote:

"They who dwell near the promontory called Bolerium are fond of strangers, and from intercourse with foreign

Gurnard Luck, a possible entry point for the Tin Traders?

merchants are civilised in their habits. These people obtain tin by skilfully working the soil which produces it. When they have formed it into cubical shapes, they convey it to certain islands lying off Britain, named Ictis. From thence the merchants purchase tin from the natives and carry it into Gaul, and journeying through Gaul, they convey their burden on horses to the outlet of the River Rhône."

The 'promontory called Bolerium' has been identified as Lands End, but 'Ictis' provides a little uncertainty, some authorities saying that this is St Michael's Mount in Cornwall, and others confusing it with Vectis, the Isle of Wight.

There seem to be one or two points here that require explanation. If the merchants came all the way from the Mediterranean by sea to collect the tin, it would seem pointless to transfer it from the mines on the mainland to St Michael's Mount. If in fact the tin was shipped from Cornwall across the Channel to Gaul, the shippers were far more likely to be local men, not Phœnicians or Greeks. Or could the trade have been overland all the way from Marseilles, in which case the merchants could have been Greek, but definitely not Phœnicians from Carthage? Another puzzling point is that Diodorous Siculus was writing before the Roman conquest of Britain, and hence possibly before the name Vectis was given to the Isle of Wight. Could the island have been called Ictis at that time?

Strabo, who was born in 66 B.C., describes the Cassiterides as "lying near the ocean towards the mouth of the Haven Artabil", and adds that formerly the Phœnicians (i.e. from Carthage) alone carried on the trade in tin, but that later the Romans took it over.

When the Romans did acquire Marseilles and the whole of France (Gaul), and were established in Britain, it is believed there was a trade route from Cornwall, over Dartmoor, to Salisbury Plain, so that it is at least possible that tin could have been brought this way, though the way would be long and tortuous. Somewhere along the route, possibly in the neighbourhood of Salisbury, it would be joined by another Roman trade route from the mineral district of the Mendip Hills where not only have ancient workings been found but pigs of lead lost by the Romans have been discovered by the road-side.

From Salisbury the road then went via the New Forest to Lepe, where traces of a Roman road heading off to the north-west have been found. Protagonists of this theory then proudly point to the fact that close to Lepe is Stansore Point, and Stanswood Bay, the Latin word *stannum* meaning tin.

From Lepe a crossing would be made to Gurnard where, until recently, there were the remains of a Roman Villa. From Gurnard, which incidentally is suggested could be derived from the Latin word *gubernalis*, the route plunges due south, across the Island along Rew Street, Gunville Road, Carisbrooke, the Priory, Nursery Lane, New Close House, Marvel Farm, Rookley, Bagwich Lane, Whitwell, and ultimately to Puckaster Cove near Niton. Many of these names are claimed to be significant – Rew Street from the French *rue*, Gunville from a town in northern France, *Gonville*, which is also on the route, and Puckaster from the Latin *castra*, a camp. In 1799 Puckaster was in fact given on a map as 'Port Castra'. Another local word which is said to be implicated is Buddle, which in mining terms is a wooden inclined trough used for washing ore.

From Puckaster the tin could then be shipped across the Channel to France, and hence by horse down south to the River Rhône and ultimately to the ancient Greek colony of Marseilles. It must be admitted that this is an interesting theory, with so many place names having an apparent connection with the trade. But the theory has been condemned by many historians as fanciful, and Helge Kokeritz, who is the acknowledged expert on the meaning of Isle of Wight place names, says the whole thing is preposterous.

Bagwich Lane, on the route across the Island.

50

Further south, passing through the village of Whitwell.

So who is right? Did the convoys once thread their way through the Island, carrying their loads of Cornish tin from Gurnard to Puckaster? Or is it just a series of coincidences that there are so many names apparently connected with the trade? Some would say that there must have been fire somewhere to have generated so much smoke!

Visiting the nest.

A NEST OF ROBINS

FIVE years ago the robins nested in our garden shed. It was very exciting. They had been nesting in the garden, and in the little wood at the back, for several years, and we have always fed them every day, along with all the other birds in the garden, so they are old friends. But to have them nesting in the shed was something special and a cause for celebration.

In the spring and summer the shed door is left open every day but closed at night, and it was fortunate that we happened to see the robins going in and out, otherwise there might have been problems. As it was I managed to shut the door but put a wedge in near the top so that it was still open a crack. It did not do the door any good but gave them enough room to squeeze in.

In the corner of the shed opposite the door is hanging a model of a favourite boat of ours, *Peradventure*. This was made for us by a friend, and when we moved here my wife cunningly constructed a box for it with a sloping roof and this we hung in the shed until such time as we could find a suitable spot for it indoors. Alas for the schemes of mice and men we have not yet found this, and the model has remained in its corner. But the robins considered it eminently suitable for their purposes and proceeded to build their nest in the angle between this box and the wall of the shed. It did not take them long, and we awaited results with a slightly increased pulse rate.

In what seemed no time at all the male robin was flying in with food in his beak, first for her, and then, as he was joined by her on the same task, for some chicks. They seemed to have enormous appetites and we felt it could not be long before they left the nest.

We were right, but not prepared for the fact that they did not immediately leave the shed. No, they found the great expanse of this 'hanger' an ideal place for practising take-offs and bumps, so that they were able to perfect their aerobatics before plunging into the harsh world of magpies, jackdaws and jays. And you should have seen the mess! House training was definitely not one of the skills learned from their parents, and our bicycles, garden tools and lawn mower suffered accordingly.

But we enjoyed it. We only ever saw three chicks at the same time but there may possibly have been more, and it was quite a thrill to see these helpless little balls of fluff develop rapidly into fully fledged birds. Nevertheless, when they finally left we breathed a great sigh of relief, cleaned up the mess, and I removed the wedge from the door. We congratulated ourselves on having raised a family of robins, and felt very superior to our neighbours.

Alas and alack, pride surely cometh before a fall, and our feeling of achievement was comparatively short lived. It was about six months later, when the summer was almost over and we were tidying up the shed, that we went to clear away the robins' old nest. In it we found six further eggs, and suddenly the full horror of the situation hit us. We had shut the door of the shed prematurely, not realizing that she was attempting to raise another brood, and we had deliberately prevented the female robin from reaching her eggs. Contrition was instant and painful; feverishly I cut a permanent square hole in the top of the door, but of course it was too late, months too late, and we had to live with our shame.

Sadly the winter passed away and spring returned, but no robins came back to investigate the shed. Could you, indeed, blame them? They still used the bird table, but reverted to nesting in the wood behind our garden. The next year it was the same, and we resigned ourselves to a nestless future as far as the robins were concerned.

And then, after two barren years, hope began to flicker and the robins began to take an interest once more. Soon they were tearing in and out with nesting material, but none of it appeared in the corner where the previous nest had been. Perhaps this corner was forever damned. On the opposite side of the shed was a shelf on which was a double row of old coffee jars containing screws, nails, tacks, etc, and all the other odds and ends that one tends to hoard in the false hope that one day they will be useful. It was on this precarious foundation they were building their nest.

Their activity became frantic, for quite two-thirds of the stuff they brought in fell off the shelf on to the bench below, and we began to get pretty nervy ourselves, silently urging them on to success. Steadily the pile grew, and it seemed incredible that two small birds could shift so much material, but it began to look as though the nest was nearing completion. And then, for the second time, we blotted our copybook. One day we inadvertently left the shed door open all day, from early morning until dusk, and when I went to close it a scene of devastation met my gaze. All the nesting material had been pulled down off the shelf together with one or two coffee jars, and the debris was scattered all over the place.

The damage must have been caused by a cat. We like to think it was some animal of doubtful parentage living in the neighbourhood, and not our own innocent little black, purring feline predator, although I suspect he would murder his grandmother if only she were small and defenceless enough. The cat next door is known to have even stronger predatory instincts, and if unmolested will crouch under our bird table for hours, hoping for a windfall. Yes, it must have been her! Fortunately no lives were lost, but it put paid to any chance of a nest of robins once again, and we gloomily felt that our garden shed would surely now be declared forbidden territory for all time.

But joy of joys! This year we did it! Spring came along, and so did the robins. This time they went for their original nesting site on top of the *Peradventure* model; this time there was no problem about free entry to the shed, the square hole was there for all to see; this time we kept the door shut against any possible marauder.

This time events ran smoothly. From my desk under the study window I was able to watch their every move, and a convenient branch of the chestnut tree provided them with a staging post which they invariably used on their way in. The nest did not take long to build, and soon the male robin was on the food run again, having apparently found an inexhaustible supply of grubs. We used the shed daily in the normal way and this did not seem to upset them. Indeed, on one occasion I met her coming out as I was going in, and

Food for hungry chicks.

First arrival. "What a strange world!"

even this did not ruffle her feathers. We had no idea how many eggs she had laid but in due course they started to hatch, and we realized there must be several mouths to feed, for both parents became very busy taking in food. Excitement grew as the time for flight neared, and I took the precaution of covering most of our possessions with plastic sheeting.

We shall never forget V.E. Day this year, for it was on this day that the first little round ball of fluff appeared on the windowsill of the shed. He was soon joined by a second, and then a third, and yet another, until four little faces were staring out at the great wide world. By this time I had been joined by my wife who drew up a chair alongside, and together we watched, enthralled, as this whole pageant of life unfolded before us.

The chicks seemed reluctant to leave the safety of the shed, and the last thing we wanted to do was to force them out into a green but cruel world, but when we saw one trying to reach the hole we thought the time had come to open the door. Keeping a sharp look-out for cats, we let them out, but the minute they had gone we found two more in the shed. These must have been later arrivals and it was a few days before they too braved the world. Once they had departed, silence descended on the shed and it reverted to being just a store for bicycles and garden equipment.

*"I **will** learn how to fly!"*

But wait a minute! Is she going to lay a second clutch? Do we have to go through all this again? Better not move that plastic sheeting just yet!

FURTHER BOOKS BY RON WINTER

COLOURFUL CHARACTERS OF THE ISLE OF WIGHT
THE ENCHANTED ISLE – *a history of the Isle of Wight*
MANOR HOUSES OF THE ISLE OF WIGHT
VILLAGE CHURCHES OF THE ISLE OF WIGHT
TRAVELLERS' JOY – *living and walking on the Isle of Wight*
"QUEEN MARY": EARLY YEARS
LONG LIVE THE "QUEEN MARY"

OTHER BOOKS AVAILABLE FROM
COACH HOUSE PUBLICATIONS LTD

ALUM BAY AND THE NEEDLES
by John C. Medland

SHIPWRECKS OF THE WIGHT
By John C. Medland

PASTORAL PILGRIMAGE
– *walks on the Isle of Wight*
written and illustrated by Victor Vivian

RED SQUIRRELS
by H. Butler and J. Norledge

ISLAND TREASURY OF VERSE
– *original illustrated verse*
by Lynn New

ILLUSTRATED TREASURY OF VERSE
– *original illustrated verse*
by Lynn New

HISTORY OF SILVER MOTOR YACHTS
– *reprint of 1920's book*
by John Bain

BEAUTY OF THE ISLE OF WIGHT

Children's Books:

THE ADVENTURES OF CHIT CHAT
– *the talking Mirror dinghy*
by Carole Hughes, illustrated by Robert Scott

ISLE OF WIGHT COLOURING BOOK

Obtainable from:

Coach House Publications Ltd, The Coach House
School Green Road, Freshwater, Isle of Wight, PO40 9BB
Telephone (01983) 755655   Fax (01983) 754683